The Touch of a Poet's Heart

By David R Marchant

The contents of this work, including, but not limited to, the accuracy of events, people, and places depicted; opinions expressed; permission to use previously published materials included; and any advice given or actions advocated are solely the responsibility of the author, who assumes all liability for said work and indemnifies the publisher against any claims stemming from publication of the work.

All Rights Reserved
Copyright © 2023 by David R Marchant

No part of this book may be reproduced or transmitted, downloaded, distributed, reverse engineered, or stored in or introduced into any information storage and retrieval system, in any form or by any means, including photocopying and recording, whether electronic or mechanical, now known or hereinafter invented without permission in writing from the publisher.

Dorrance Publishing Co
585 Alpha Drive
Suite 103
Pittsburgh, PA 15238
Visit our website at *www.dorrancebookstore.com*

ISBN: 979-8-88729-408-7
eISBN: 979-8-88729-908-2

*All of my poems are original.
Many were written under my penname, "Poet Doctor."*

*Unless otherwise noted, these poems were written
and inspired by my ex-wife, my dear friends,
and my deep religious beliefs.*

*They were also written and inspired by my life's work
and experience as a mental health provider,
as well as my own personal journey,
and ongoing recovery from PTSD.*

*I've also added two poems that I wrote many years ago
while in high school and college.*

To my children, Holly, Abbey, and Brady, thank you for always believing in me and encouraging me to publish this book. You have always believed in me and motivated me to get better and BE better. My hope is that this book will bless you and our family for generations to come.

To my mother and stepfather, you have always inspired me to reach for my dreams and never let adversity keep me from achieving them. Thank you for being my greatest examples of how that it is done.

To my Aunt Roma, thank you for always encouraging me in my life. I will miss the look on your face every time I shared one of my poems with you. I know you would have cherished having your own copy of this book.

Preface

  In the Summer of 2021, I became a published poet for the first time in my life. Two poems about my journey with PTSD were published in *Veterans Voices Magazine.* In 2022, three more poems with the same theme were also published in the same magazine. Achieving this milestone helped motivate me to put this collection together.

  My collection of poetry includes poems about romance, love, beauty, faith, coping with grief, and friendship. I have also shared very personal poems about coping with PTSD, finding hope, support, and persevering towards recovery. Hopefully, they will help inspire others facing similar challenges in their life to find the courage they need to keep fighting until they are overcome.

  The majority of my poems are written in the "Free Verse" style of poetry. This writing form, as described by *Writers.com*, "doesn't rely on any particular, meter, or rhyme scheme, yet still conveys powerful feelings and ideas." (www.writers.com).

  My hope is that you, as the reader, will understand that each break and return of a stanza were written intentionally to help convey to the reader, the same emotion I was feeling at the time they were written. It was with that idea in mind that the title of this book was inspired.

  I hope you enjoy reading them just as much as I enjoyed writing them.

- DM/Poet Doctor

David R Marchant

The Light Within

There's a light within her
and I knew immediately
the moment I saw her
my life would never be the same
until she shared that light with me

This light is magnified when
she smiles or when I'm near her
in how she makes me feel
whenever I hold her close to me
fueling my desire to love her more

Now I spend my days making sure
her light radiates even brighter
through my words, my promises
and that look from me that
tells her daily my heart is hers

When her light glows brightest
it strengthens my resolve
to always make sure it never
dims or is extinguished
always strengthened by mine

The Touch *of a* Poet's Heart

A Part Of Me

I keep my heart locked away
only a few special people
have ever been able
to find their way inside

You are one of them

What we have is special
a truly amazing connection
my heart was yours
with no questions or reservations

You have become a part of me

Now that part of my heart
will forever be yours

She Is The One

She is the one
my heart longs for
the one who
fills my dreams

The one that
I'm thinking about
whenever I'm smiling

She is the one
I want to hold
the one whose
lips I crave

Forever hold in my arms
and completely give
my heart to

A woman who is worthy
of being cherished
the one I get to say
I love you to
every single day

The Touch of a Poet's Heart

Her True Beauty

It's in the curve of her face
into those perfect lips
where I see her true beauty
but it's in her eyes
that her true secret is hidden.

She is not easy to pursue
If she lets you in
your whole soul will feel it
then she will give you
everything your heart
could ever want or desire

David R Marchant

Can You Tell Me Why

Can you tell me why
the deepest part of my soul
the place I believed
was forever broken…
always comes alive
whenever
I am with you

Was it chance we met
or was it actually serendipity
that brought us together
Whatever the reason…
I can't ever
imagine
my life without you

In My Eyes

I see that look in your eyes
the one that comes
every time you stand in
front of the mirror

I know what your eyes see
and what your mind is saying

But oh how your beauty
shines from in and out of you
and radiates over every part of me

I wish you could see exactly
what my eyes see
my heart feels
and what my soul treasures

You are the one I think about
the woman I desire
the one… who captured my soul

In my eyes you will always be
perfect and truly beautiful

David R Marchant

For Her

Every day I strive to
　make her smile
Because her eyes and her smile
light up my entire world
and fill my heart
　with joy

My words and my thoughts
　are purposely given
To help her know and understand
that she is cared for
with my entire soul
　and cherished

But more than that
　she is valued
A rare priceless pearl among pearls
a treasure more valuable
than all other treasures
　on Earth

So I strive every day
to always make sure
that her heart also beats for me

The Touch of a Poet's Heart

Every Time

Every time
I think of her
the pain of her leaving
wells up inside me

Now
wherever I go
I can't escape the memories
of our life together

She
is so deeply
intertwined into my soul
I can't let go

How
do I begin
to move on alone
without her love

Eternity
can only exist
with her and I together
hand in hand

Unaware

I see her
but she is unaware
that I am near
until my arms
encircle her from behind
then pull her close
and she feels
the warmth of my breath
on her neck

She is breathless
shivering
anticipating my kiss
breathless from my embrace
the touch of my lips
knees weak
melting from my touch
eager for more

Passionate Kiss

I lean in close
my hand touches your face
in my eyes you see
my love for you
your eyes close
then the space between us
disappears
our lips softly touch
then part so our tongues
can dance together

We both feel the other's
heart racing
hands are now
exploring each other
our mutual desire
is more than evident
neither one of us can
deny the fire growing
inside of us
destined to be fulfilled

David R Marchant

I Wonder If She Knows

I wonder if she knows
why I choose her every day
The answer is simple
because her smile
brings joy into my life
Her presence brings me peace
So how could
I choose anyone else

The Touch of a *Poet's Heart*

There's Never Been Anyone

There's never been anyone
who held my heart
like she did
and now I wonder
if anyone ever will again

It happened so quickly
love at first sight
it was predestined
from that first moment
all my heart was hers

Two souls completely given
a connection others envied
forged in love
a bond so great
only death could break it

But now she's gone
my life is empty
our love lost
the bond is broken
our chance for eternity shattered

Oh how my heart yearns
to hold her again
touch her face
kiss her lips
feel our love once again

David R Marchant

A Smile Like No Other

She has a smile like no other
like a ray of sunshine
it warms my soul and
quiets my demons
letting me know that
everything will be alright

From the moment we said hello
we both could sense that
what we had was special
like it was always
meant to be like this
a deep meaningful connection

I crave her presence every day
need to feel her close to me
give her reasons to smile
tell her she is beautiful
and make her feel loved

The **Touch** *of a* **Poet's Heart**

Unspoken

There never seem to be
enough words
to tell you how I feel
or enough words
to describe your smile
or what it does to me
when I see it

But your true beauty comes
from within
I see it in your eyes
feel it deep inside me
echoed in emotions
shared daily between the
two of us

My hands can't physically
touch your body
so my words will act as proxy
to capture the heart
and inspire your mind
my intent understood
your heart protected

My Forever Love

When I am with her
my heart fills with emotions
that I am powerless to control
the truest form of love
freely given

When she looks at me
my eyes see what my heart
has always understood
her eternal love is
never wavering

When I hold her in my arms
all my worries disappear
replaced with a calm assurance
that any challenge
can be overcome

She is and will forever be
the one whose love
I work every day to deserve
love without limits
joy everlasting

My Crush

I need her next to me
to smell her perfume
touch her softy
look into her eyes
put my arms around her
feel her skin close to mine

I long to taste her lips
show my feelings
reconnect with her heart
hear her speak my name
when I pull her in close
and melt her with my kiss

She will always be my crush
the one I desire the most
a woman like no other
my dream and my wish
but distance separates
a love meant to be

For this moment I'm content
to keep her in my heart
aware we cannot be together
my feelings and desires for her
must be kept to myself
until we are together again

David R Marchant

In Her Arms Of Love

One smile from her
and my heart skips
all my worries gone
overpowered by
her unending beauty

She is the one
who has my heart
now and forever
willingly given
and forever promised

I long to have her
with me by my side
to give all my heart to
surrounded in
her arms of love

Her love is necessary
like the air I breathe
she gives me hope
effortlessly and
I am forever grateful

Just One Glimpse

Her smile never stops
but oh her eyes can
take my breath away
she has beauty that's
far more than physical
it radiates from everywhere

Just one glimpse of her
would change your life
but a moment with her
is more transformative
forever craving her presence
constantly wishing for much more

David R Marchant

How Many Ways

How many ways can I say
that you're the one
my angel from heaven
the only woman
that I could ever want
to share my life with

Because what we have
could never be duplicated
no one will ever have
your smile or your eyes
or that look you give me
when I say I love you

No one could ever replace
the memories we've built
over a lifetime of love
no one could make me
feel the way I do
when you walk into a room

The Touch of a Poet's Heart

How could any woman
in a brief moment, ever
give me what you have;
your heart, your mind
or your ability to love me
despite all my weaknesses

I am yours completely
yesterday, today, and forever
my love for you is infinite
immeasurable and eternal
there will never be a reason
to doubt that I am yours

David R Marchant

True Beauty

She can light up a room
with just her smile
distracting my attention
and involuntarily my gaze
gracefully glides
over the rest of her

She is the textbook definition
of true beauty, her
presence is enough but
her eyes, smile
and gorgeous curves
deserve attention as well

She is the kind of woman
men dream about
give poets inspiration
novelists their heroine
and is the muse for
a musicians instrument

She is worth every effort
a woman worthy of
adoration and celebration
a precious gift
a rare and priceless gem
a challenge to pursue

If She Only Knew

If she only knew how much
she crosses my mind in a day
or how her smile makes me
weak in the knees every time
would she understand what I feel

My heart knows she will
never be mine completely
but my thoughts, my desires
and my dreams are all of her
could she believe this to be true

I'm content with what we have
how she calms my demons
inspires my innermost desires
my need to fuel hers too
when in reality we fuel each other's

I'm driven to make her smile
but it's so much more than that
I want her to feel loved, appreciated
and more importantly beautiful
the way my life is because of her

David R Marchant

I Still See Her

I still see her
in quiet moments
during my day
and when I drift off to sleep

Yet my memory of that experience
is already beginning to fade

For a brief instant
I held you
in my arms again
the intensity of our love reunited

Oh how I wanted to stay
but it wasn't my time

So here I am once again
trying to live
my life without you
knowing my angel is in heaven

Waiting for that day when
we will be reunited again

(Inspired by a dream)

The Touch of a Poet's Heart

Destined

At that moment
you realize
that her eyes
and smile
have become
permanently imprinted
on your soul

But now
no matter what you do
to try to let her go
you will never
be able to escape them

They are
destined to haunt
your memories
for the rest of forever

Captivated

In the beginning
he was captivated
by her smile
but somewhere during
the journey
he fell in love
with her soul

The Touch of a Poet's Heart

I Never Wanted

I never wanted
to love again
I never wanted to
feel again
or experience that much
pain again
So I locked
that part of my heart away

Then she came
into my life
and suddenly everything
was different
The lock was broken
her soul
penetrated every inch
of my once broken heart

How I want her to be mine
but for now
I can only be in love with her
from a distance……

One Look

She defines beauty
her body is indeed
magnificent
but she is beautiful
for much more than that

Just one look at her
will leave you breathless
wishing she was yours
to behold
every day

A Map Of Her Neck

I want to make a map of her neck
slowly trace every inch
discover the places
that stimulate
the areas the make her body squirm
the one that signals
her mind that she is ready

When I am done creating
I will make the journey again
this time with my lips and tongue
so I can leave her
breathless
and desperate for more

All That Glitters

When the limo arrives
the door opens
and the cameras flash
then everyone's attention
is focused on her
they've been waiting
for this moment
when their star emerges
her shoes glitter
in the lights

Her thighs are smooth
then their first glimpse
of her golden gown
as she steps
onto the curb then
walks the red carpet
she sparkles in the night
dressed to kill

The Touch of a Poet's Heart

Walking with confidence
in an expensive dress
immaculate nails
dangling gold and diamonds
creating the image
of success to the crowd

But the smile
tells them everything
she is much more than
what she is wearing
her most precious jewel
is the one on the inside
a heart of infinite worth
cherished by the one who
she gave it too

Perfect In Polka Dots

She puts it on
when she wants to feel
classically beautiful
channeling her inner
Grace, Audrey, Julia,
or Princess Di

But sometimes she wears it
when she is feeling
playful and flirty like
Kate, Emily, Katy,
or Scarlett Jo

Truthfully, the reason
has nothing to do with
the who or the why...
she wears polka dots
for one reason

Because she loves them

The Touch of a Poet's Heart

Calm The Storm In Me

I need Him in my life
to quiet my soul
heal my broken heart
forgive my sins
bear me up
wrap me in His arms of love
and calm the storm in me

Why I Pray

Father, in the quiet night
I am calling, I am pleading
it's your wisdom I am seeking
my burden is heavy
can you take it away
Father, hear me as I pray

Father, in the quiet night
I am waiting, I am listening
for your answer to my pleading
my faith is tested
I won't go astray
Father, hear me as I pray

Father, help me, hear me
bless me, heal me
take me in thy warm embrace
give me strength to live each day
Father, this is why I pray

The Touch of a Poet's Heart

Father, your answer comes
as a witness and a burning
to my troubled heart confirming
your Spirit speaks
and I obey
Father, this is why I pray

Oh Father, help me, hear me
bless me, heal me
take me in thy warm embrace
give me strength
to live each day
Father, this is why I pray

This poem was edited to fit the music for the song
"Why I Pray" music by Aaron Waite.

(Published in Hymns Today Summer Edition 2013)

David R Marchant

Rescue Me

When I was younger
I lost my way
but then I met you
and the power of your love
Rescued me

Many years passed by
I lost my way again
but you never strayed
and the power of your love
rescued me

Now here I am again
I've lost my way
I'm out of chances
now I need my Savior's love
to rescue me

My life is empty without you
and I don't know
if I can do this alone
but with His love I know
I can be rescued

The Touch of a Poet's Heart

When He Sees Me Wake

Each morning when I wake I know
that Satan and his foes
are standing outside my door again
to tempt me more and more

On my knees I start my day with prayer
the scriptures I will read
my armor must be strong you know
to keep him far from me

With faith I know I am not alone
my testimony strong and pure
though Evil tries to break my will
my victory will be assured

Satan's power will ultimately weaken
defeated, He will slow his pace
vanquished by this Warrior
whose courage comes with faith

Satan knows that a righteous man
has a will he cannot break
I pray His knees will shake with fear
when he sees me wake

David R Marchant

A Cemetery On A Hill

Winter Quarters is a place
where Pioneers came to heal
it is also where they left their dead
at a cemetery on a hill

As a child I often came
to see this sacred place
I walked the grounds, I knelt to pray
the Lord's Spirit to embrace

Now today when I return
to walk and pray and feel
a special building has been raised
near this cemetery on a hill

The Touch of a Poet's Heart

The Temple of our Holy Lord
now stands as a shining testament
a place of honor has been dedicated
as a reward for their torment

I pay them honor every time I go
to covenant and know God's will
His Spirit fills that sacred place
near their cemetery on a hill

(written after viewing the Winter Quarters Temple in Omaha Nebraska 2004)

David R Marchant

She Is The Angel

She is the angel
that God sent to me
to guide my way
on this difficult journey

She is the answer
to a fervent prayer
given by His servant
with faith He is there

She is my comforter
helps soothe my soul
inspired by the Savior
to heal me, her goal

She follows her heart
her words comfort me
while holding my hand
and helps me to see

I am not broken
with confidence I'll proceed
on this journey forward
my expectation to succeed

(This poem was written as a thank you gift for one of the therapists that helped me during my journey of healing and recovery. Jessica, there are not enough words to express my gratitude for your help.)

The Touch of a Poet's Heart

His Love Will Rescue You

As the Savior knelt in Gethsemane
our sins he freely chose to bear
He did not ask His Father why
or wonder if He were there

Later when He hung on the cross
in pain, a lesson He did share
He never cursed His Father's name
or doubt if He were there

As others try to get through life
faced with pain and in despair
they ask why and curse His name
not believing He is there

In my life I know I will be tested
His example helps guide my prayers
by seeking Him and enduring well
I know He will be there

Your Father waits for you to kneel
and pray for strength, your pain to heal
the trials lesson you must learn
your burden lifted, a promise true
His love will rescue you

David R Marchant

Carry It For You

I know the weight
you're feeling inside
the pain in your heart
a world now untied
there are no words
that could ever
ease you through
but know this my friend
this burden you feel
I would carry it for you

(For a dear friend and her family)

The Touch of a Poet's Heart

I Wish I Could Tell You

I wish I could tell you
it doesn't hurt
because it does
I wish I could tell you
the tears will stop
because they won't
I wish I could tell you
you'll never stop missing them
because you will

What I can tell you
is that the pain
will get better
what I can tell you
is that the tears
won't be as frequent
what I can tell you
is you'll still miss them
but only the good things

David R Marchant

Let your tears flow
feel your emotions
don't run from them
reach out to the those
who care for you
hold them close
then push forward
live your life to honor them
you are strong, you can do this

(For those grieving the loss of a loved one)

The Touch of a Poet's Heart

The Glow Of The Moon

The glow of the moon
brings light to the water
casting a shadow
of brilliant blue hues
across the lake
framed in pitch black
by the surrounding landscape

Like a sheet of glass
the water is still and calm
the only music
comes from the forest
hand in hand
we walk the shoreline
taking in the moment together

The chill of the night
draws you into my arms
my body warms
makes you feel safe
our eyes connect
the kiss overwhelms, electrifies
and takes your breath away

David R Marchant

A Warrior In Me

Why must I bear this burden
that cripples me to my knees
my strength at this moment
shattered
like it was only an illusion
two steps forward
then ten steps back
my demons in full control
I'm lost, broken
searching desperately for hope
a reason to continue
fighting the thoughts
to just surrender
and release myself from this pain

But I can't
there are those who
depend on me
the easy way out
won't be easy for them
there's a Warrior in me
proven in battle
soon he will rise again
and claw his way back

(Published in Veteran Voices Magazine in 2021)

The Touch of a Poet's Heart

Not All Wounds Are Visible

I am a Warrior
who overcame his fears
served with distinction
returned with Honor

But the person I was before
will never be the same
I carry scars on the outside
that time has healed

But there are others
that haunt my memories
far more difficult to overcome
but I will never give up the fight

(Published in Veteran Voices Magazine in 2022)

David R Marchant

True Heroes

The smoke has cleared
the battle over and the wall
finally traversed
once again I'm on the other side
weary, but stronger from the fight
the Warrior in me
stands victorious
yet ever aware
the battle was not won
single handedly
there were others
who fought with me
always at my side
never allowing me to give up
while the battle raged
inside me.

In my eyes…
they are the true Heroes.

(Published in Veteran Voices Magazine in 2021)

That Look

There it is
that look in your eyes
distant
empty of emotion
the one
masking the memories
of a battlefield
far, far away

I recognize it
because I have seen it
before
staring back
at me in the mirror
absent of feeling
devoid of all hope
lost and alone

David R Marchant

I've been there
sat in a similar chair
desperate
for answers
fighting alone
always looking back
then help was offered
my journey began

You'll need courage
to make this same journey
determination
eyes forward
never looking back
willingness to trust
let me help you
you're not alone

(Published in Veterans Voices Magazine in 2022. Winner of the Sue and Sally Hughes Memorial Award for the Fall 2022 issue of this same publication.)

But Not Alone

I turn the page on
my calendar
it's March 1st again
I know what stands
in front of me
31 days
one giant wall
seemingly impossible
to climb
it strikes fear through
every part of me
so many painful memories
too many losses
including
the ONE
a love so amazing
I can't let it go
and so I must battle
one foot in front of the other
head held high
I can do this...

but not alone

Demons In The Dark

I

Demons in the dark
I feel your presence
but know
that I am a warrior
and I do not fight alone
I will be victorious

II

Demons in the dark
you fought very well
but not enough to defeat me
retreat back to where you came from

I will always fight
I'm skilled in battle
so if you return, know
I will keep fighting until my last breath

This Road I'm On

This road I'm on is hard
but there's no option
for me to turn back

The painful memories I have buried
have taken a toll
on those that I love

But more so on myself

I have to face my deepest fears
tear open the scars
of my traumatic experiences

Feel the emotions and the pain
that I buried inside
and tried to forget

This journey will be difficult
but I don't have to
take it by myself

This road I'm on can only
go in one direction
and that's straight ahead

(Published in Veterans Voices Magazine in 2022)

David R Marchant

For Dad

(written in 1979)

The Seasons have passed
we have grown
you have missed them
how could you have known
a thousand miles apart
we still remembered
our time with you Dad
like it was yesterday

I remember those nights
I laid thinking
of the things we used to do
how could I have known
every night and every day
I still remember
the fun we used to have
like it was yesterday

The Touch of a Poet's Heart

Oh how I wish
that we could start again
just remember days gone past
just me and my dad

The road has been tough
but He has led me
down the straight and narrow
only God could have known

Though the years were long and hard
God still remembers
the love that we have
together, forever

David R Marchant

You Are The One

(Written in 1979)

You are the one
I asked into my life
although it wasn't easy
it worked out right

Love was just beginning
but now it has to end
you are moving away
so this plea I send

I wish you didn't have to leave
my life will be empty without you
let me tell you one more time
I will always love you

Now my hope for the future
is that we will meet again
for a second chance at love
I will wait until eternity ends

Well I guess this is it then
I hope you feel the same too
promise you will not forget
I will always love you

(A poem written for someone special in high school)